MANÉ

RULES

> **Hi,** pleased to meet you.

> We hope you enjoy our book about Sadio Mané!

> I'm **VARbot** with all the facts and stats!

SIMON

DAN

WELBECK

VAR

THIS IS A WELBECK CHILDREN'S BOOK
Published in 2021 by Welbeck Children's Books Limited
An imprint of the Welbeck Publishing Group
20 Mortimer Street, London W1T 3JW
Text © 2021 Simon Mugford
Design & Illustration © 2021 Dan Green
ISBN: 978-1-78312-641-5

Writer: Simon Mugford
Designer and Illustrator: Dan Green
Design manager: Sam James
Executive editor: Suhel Ahmed
Production: Arlene Alexander

A catalogue record for this book is available from the British Library.

Printed in the UK
10 9 8 7 6 5 4 3 2 1

Statistics and records correct as of June 2021

FOOTBALL SUPERSTARS

MANÉ

RULES

SIMON MUGFORD   DAN GREEN

CONTENTS

CHAPTER 1

AMAZING MANÉ

MANÉ, MANÉ!

Say hello to **Sadio Mané** - one of the very best footballers in the world. **Liverpool's** quiet and shy **wonder on the wing** is a **Premier League** and **Champions League** winner who **WOWS** the fans with his

LIGHTNING SPEED AND SUPER SKILLS.

JUST WHAT IS IT THAT MAKES
SADIO MANÉ SO GOOD?

Speed
One of quickest players in the game, he flies past his opponents.

Finishing
Excels at picking up passes and firing the ball home.

Trickery
Outwits defenders with lightning-fast twists and turns.

Cool and calm
Mané's quiet personality helps him handle the pressure.

GOALS! GOALS! GOALS!
Best of all, Mané scores goals – lots and lots of them!

MANÉ IN NUMBERS

Let's break down **Sadio Mané's career** so far **in numbers:**

400 . . . career appearances

169 . . . career goals

95 . . . PREMIER LEAGUE goals

1 . . . PREMIER LEAGUE title

MANÉ I.D.

NAME: *Sadio Mané*

NICKNAME:
*'Ronaldinho',
'Ballonbuwa'
(The Ball Wizard)*

DATE OF BIRTH:
10 April 1992

PLACE OF BIRTH: *Sedhiou, Senegal*

HEIGHT: *1.74 m*

POSITION: *Left winger / forward*

CLUBS: *Metz, Red Bull Salzburg,
Southampton, Liverpool*

NATIONAL TEAM: *Senegal*

LEFT OR RIGHT-FOOTED: *Right*

CHAPTER 2

BAMBALI BOY

Sadio Mané is from **Senegal,** a country on the **west coast of Africa**. He was born in **1992** and grew up in the tiny village of **Bambali.**

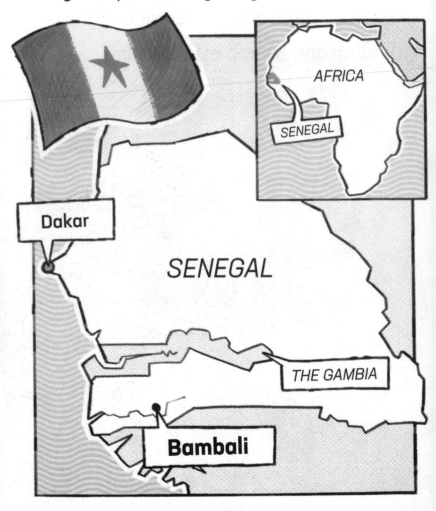

Senegal is famous for its **music,** **storytellers** and amazing **food.**

Everyone loves football in Senegal but the **number one sport is wrestling.**

There wasn't much to do in Bambali for young Sadio. He went to **school.**

He went to the **mosque.**

He **worked** in the fields to help his family.

Sadio didn't want to be a **fisherman** or a **farmer** like others living in Bambali. He wanted to play –

FOOTBALL!

TOK!

When Sadio was very little, he would practise kicking anything he could find - stones, tin cans, even **grapefruit!**

There were no **football pitches** in Bambali.

The boys in the village had to play in the streets.

Soon, the quiet and shy
little Sadio plucked up
the courage to join them.

And Sadio wasn't just **good** at football.

HE WAS FANTASTIC AT FOOTBALL!

BOP!

ZOOM!

He dribbled through
the streets, passed to
his team-mates . . .

. . . and scored
amazing goals!

BOOM!

None of the other boys controlled the ball
as well as Mané. In Bambali, they called him
BALLONBUWA - the **'Ball Wizard'**.

A terrible thing happened when Sadio was just **seven years old.** His father died suddenly. But Sadio had a **very big family.**

His aunts and uncles - almost the **entire village** - would look after him.

And he has **always** remembered this.

CHAPTER 3

LEARNING LESSONS

Sadio would have played football **all the time** if he could. But his family wanted him to **focus on school** and his studies.

IT'S IMPORTANT YOU GET A GOOD EDUCATION, SADIO.

They did not see how **SERIOUS** he was about becoming a footballer.

When he was allowed to play football, Sadio was getting **better** and **BETTER!**

His **pace,** control, trickery and goals earned him another nickname, **'Ronaldinho'**, after Barcelona's Brazilian star of the time.

Sadio knew there was **NO WAY** he would be **scouted** playing in the streets of Bambali.

So when he was 15, with the help of a friend, he ran away to **Dakar,** Senegal's capital city. His idea was to have a trial for a team there.

Dakar

It was a long journey of more than 400 km.

THE GAMBIA

Bambali

But that didn't work! His family soon found him and brought him home.

WE'VE BEEN **WORRIED** ABOUT YOU. DON'T EVER DO THAT AGAIN!

Sadio agreed a **plan** with his family: he would spend another **year at school**, then he could follow his **football dream**.

CHAPTER 4

SADIO'S HEROES

2002 was a big year for the Senegal national football team - they qualified for the World Cup **for the first time ever.**

In Bambali, Sadio and his friends gathered around a TV to watch Senegal play **France,** the reigning champions.

Incredibly, Senegal scored in the first half and held on for a **1–0 win.** The whole village celebrated wildly!

Senegal went all the way to the **quarter-finals!**

SENEGAL STARS

Almost all of the Senegalese stars of **2002** played for teams in Europe. They were living Sadio's dream

El Hadji Diouf

Great striker with a bad temper, he played for top clubs in France, England and Scotland.

Henri Camara

Striker best known in England for his Premier League goal-scoring with Wigan Athletic.

Papa Bouba Diop

Midfielder or centre-back, famous for scoring the goal against France in 2002.

Salif Diao

Defensive midfielder who began his career at Monaco, followed by spells with Liverpool and Stoke City.

In 2005, **Liverpool** played **AC Milan** in the **Champions League final.**

It looked like it was **all over** for Liverpool at half-time – they were **losing 3–0.**

But they scored **THREE** goals in the second half and won the penalty shootout! It was the most **amazing match** Sadio had seen – and now he was a **Liverpool fan!**

LIV-ER-POOL, LIV-ER-POOL!

"WATCHING THAT (THE 2002 WORLD CUP) MADE ME ABSOLUTELY DETERMINED THAT ONE DAY I WOULD DO WHAT THAT TEAM DID."

Sadio Mané

Sadio's uncle took him back to **Dakar** when he was 16. He was going for a trial with **Génération Foot,** a football academy in the capital city.

We missed the bus!

Don't worry, we can take da-kar!

40

At the trial, Sadio was wearing the same **battered old boots** he wore in **Bambali.** He saw the other boys in their **smart boots and kit** and felt very nervous!

How could he compete?

But Sadio didn't need to worry once he was on the pitch.

He **ran** . . .

. . . **passed**

TAP!

. . . and scored!

BOOM!

The Ball Wizard from Bambali had wowed

the scouts of **Génération Foot**.

THIS KID IS THE
REAL DEAL!

43

It took a while for the shy village kid to settle in the **big city**, but his **amazing football skills** soon won him **lots of friends**.

Each year, Génération Foot's **two best players** were selected for a trial at **FC Metz,** a top club in **France.**

Was Sadio getting closer to his dream of **playing in Europe?**

"I SAW IN HIM THE QUALITIES OF A TOP-LEVEL PLAYER – SPEED, DRIBBLING, AN ABILITY TO BEAT DEFENCES, LINK-UP PLAY."

Jules Boucher, Sadio's coach at Génération Foot

CHAPTER 6

METZ MAN

Before he knew it, Sadio was travelling **5000 kilometres** to begin a new life in France.

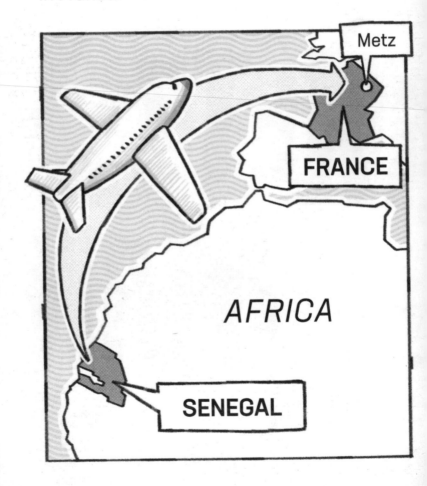

Metz was **VERY** different to Dakar. Senegal was hot and sunny almost all of the time. But in northeast France it was cold, wet and **very windy!**

Soon after he arrived at Metz, Sadio had a **serious injury,** but he didn't say anything. He was afraid he would be **sent home!**

OOOOW!

When the coach from Génération Foot
came to see how he was doing, he knew
something was wrong.

Sadio spent months recovering from his injury. It was a tough time, but his new friend **Kalidou Koulibaly**, whose family came from Senegal, looked after him.

KALIDOU KOULIBALY

Koulibaly is now the **captain of Senegal.**

When he was **fit again,** everyone at Metz saw what an **amazing** player he was. But unfortunately Mané - and Koulibaly - couldn't stop the club being **relegated** at the end of the season!

It was not the start in Europe he had hoped for.

MANÉ AT METZ

GAMES	GOALS	ASSISTS
23	2	1

"THAT PERIOD OF MY LIFE, IT GOT ME TO WHERE I AM NOW."

Sadio Mané on his time at Metz

In **2012,** Mané was a **rising star** in Senegalese football. When he made his debut in a friendly against **Morocco,** soon after turning 20, Sadio couldn't be prouder.

And he set up Senegal's winning goal!

In his next match, a World Cup qualifier against **Liberia,** he scored his first goal for Senegal.

BOOM!

Senegal are known as
'**The Lions of Teranga**'.
Err, nice kitty!

GRRR!

Senegal qualified for the **2012 Olympics** and Mané was in the squad. It was an incredible honour.

Sadio thought he was dreaming as they played host nation **Great Britain** at Old Trafford.

And in front of a **75,000** crowd at **Wembley,** Senegal won **2–0** against a Uruguay side that included **Luis Suárez** and **Edinson Cavani.**

AWESOME!

At the **2017 Africa Cup of Nations,**
Mané scored against Tunisia and Zimbabwe,
helping to set up a **quarter-final**
against **Cameroon.**

The game went to a penalty shoot-out . . .
Sadio was the last penalty taker.

But the Cameroon keeper **saved it!**

Mané was **devastated.**

Two years later, Senegal went all the way to the **final** – their first since **2002.** But it was not to be for Mané and the Lions of Teranga as they lost **1–0** to **Algeria.**

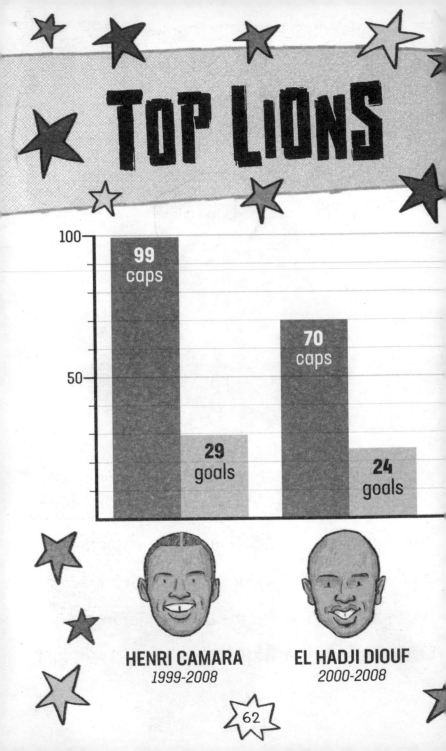

TOP LIONS

99 caps

70 caps

29 goals

24 goals

100

50

HENRI CAMARA
1999-2008

EL HADJI DIOUF
2000-2008

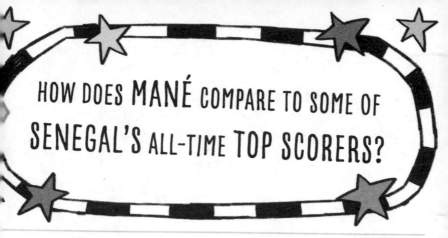

HOW DOES MANÉ COMPARE TO SOME OF SENEGAL'S ALL-TIME TOP SCORERS?

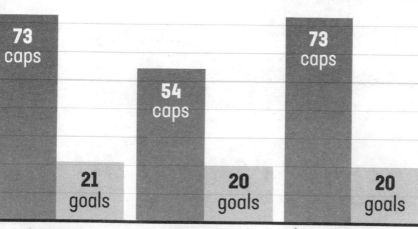

73 caps

54 caps

73 caps

21 goals

20 goals

20 goals

SADIO MANÉ
2012-

MAMADOU NIANG
2002-12

JULES BOCANDÉ
1979-93

63

At the **2018 World Cup,** Mané was the team captain. Senegal were in a **VERY** tight group where they beat **Poland** (yay), drew with **Japan** (Mané scored) but lost to **Colombia** (boo!)

SADIO'S SENEGAL RECORD

CAPS	GOALS	ASSISTS
75	23	17

CHAPTER 8

AUSTRIAN ADVENTURE

When Metz were relegated to the **French Third Division** in 2012, they put their best players up for sale.

Sadio was the very **BEST** player of all. So when the Austrian club **Red Bull Salzburg** offered **£3 MILLION,** that was it – Mané was on the move again!

FOOTBALL CLUB DE METZ

Salzburg is a very beautiful city, famous for

... **its Alpine scenery**

... **Mozart**

... **and The Sound of Music**

For Mané, it was **even colder** than Metz
and very, very different from home.

But Red Bull Salzburg had **big plans** for the
future. Sadio was **VERY** excited to be there.

DEBUT SEASON

30 SEPTEMBER 2012

AUSTRIAN BUNDESLIGA

RB SALZBURG 3-2 STURM GRAZ

*Mané's first start for Salzburg. First he set up an equalizer and then scored an **awesome** solo goal two minutes later! Graz pulled one back, only for Sadio to head home a **late winner.** Salzburg's new hero had arrived.*

WAP!

70

31 OCTOBER 2012

AUSTRIAN CUP ROUND OF 16

SC KALSDORF 1-3 RB SALZBURG

*Sadio netted all three goals in this cup tie to record his **first professional hat-trick.***

15 DECEMBER 2012

AUSTRIAN BUNDESLIGA

RB SALZBURG 7-0 SV MATTERSBURG

*Mane's second **hat-trick** of the season came in this seven-goal demolition – **BOOM!***

BEATING BAYERN

When Salzburg played a friendly against German giants **Bayern Munich** in 2014, it was a chance for Sadio to show off his skills against some of best in the business, such as . . .

Thrilling forward
Thomas Müller . . .

Midfield magician
Toni Kroos . . .

And goalkeeping great **Manuel Neuer**.

Mané was **outstanding**. He scored the first goal, won a penalty for the second and assisted the third. Salzburg won **3–0!**

Bayern manager **Pep Guardiola** was so impressed, he wanted to sign Sadio on the spot!

WOW!

DOUBLE DUTCH

Salzburg were in the **Europa League** in **2013–14** and faced top Dutch side **Ajax** in the knockout stage.

In the **first leg** he scored the second of **THREE** goals.

And in the **second leg** he fired home
(between the goalkeeper's legs) and set up
the winner. **YES!**

MANÉ'S EUROPEAN **FOOTBALL DREAM** HAD COME TRUE.

Mané picked up his first **TWO TROPHIES** with Salzburg in **2014** as they won the **Bundesliga** and **Austrian Cup** double. Sadio was flying high in the Alps!

Bundesliga Trophy

Austrian Cup

MANÉ'S SALZBURG RECORD

SEASON	GAMES	GOALS	ASSISTS
2012-13	29	19	10
2013-14	50	23	18
2014-15	8	3	4

CHAPTER 9

PREMIER CLASS

While Sadio was making his mark at Salzburg, the **Borussia Dortmund** manager **Jürgen Klopp** became a big fan.

But Sadio didn't move to Germany.

Spartak Moscow were ready to pay **BIG** money to sign him, but Mané didn't go to **Russia** either.

Instead, he was heading for England – and the **Premier League**.

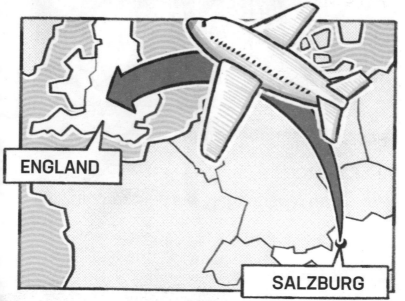

Sadio joined **Southampton** in **2014** for an estimated fee of **£11 MILLION.**

A new chapter had begun.

Mané won a penalty on his debut against **QPR**, then scored his first goal to beat **Stoke City** 1-0.

Over Christmas, Sadio scored **THREE in THREE** games, including goals against **Chelsea** and **Arsenal.**

WHOMP!

Southampton finished **seventh** in Sadio's first season – then their highest place in the **Premier League.**

HAT-TRICK MAGIC

16 MAY 2015

PREMIER LEAGUE

SOUTHAMPTON 6-1 ASTON VILLA

*Sadio opened the scoring after 13 MINUTES, then netted again - and **AGAIN.** His three strikes in **TWO minutes and 56 seconds** is the **fastest hat-trick** in Premier League history.*

TOP FIVE *FASTEST* PREMIER LEAGUE *HAT-TRICKS*

SADIO MANÉ
2015

2 MIN 56 SECS

ROBBIE FOWLER
1994

4 MIN 33 SECS

JERMAINE DEFOE
2009

7 MIN

GABRIEL AGBONLAHOR
2008

7 MIN

SERGIO AGÜERO
2015

8 MIN

3 OCTOBER 2015

PREMIER LEAGUE

CHELSEA 1-3 SOUTHAMPTON

*Southampton had drawn level just before half-time, then Sadio scored to put them 2-1 up. He also provided an assist for the third goal – and was **Man of the Match!***

20 MARCH 2016

PREMIER LEAGUE

SOUTHAMPTON 3-2 LIVERPOOL

*The Saints were trailing 2-0, before Mané inspired a late comeback, scoring **TWICE,** including the all-important winner!*

1 MAY 2016

PREMIER LEAGUE

SOUTHAMPTON 4-2 MAN CITY

*Mané's amazing hat-trick leads to another stunning win over a big club - **AWESOME!***

Mané was Southampton's top scorer, helping them finish **SIXTH** that season.

MANÉ AT SOUTHAMPTON

SEASON	GAMES	GOALS	ASSISTS
2014-15	32	10	5
2015-16	43	15	9

CHAPTER 10

MANÉ THE RED

Sadio secretly hoped that playing for Southampton might lead to a **move** to a REALLY big club. It came in the summer of 2016 when he joined **Liverpool** for

£34 MILLION.

Jürgen Klopp had finally got his man!

Mané was the **most expensive** African player.

Sadio joined Brazilians **Philippe Coutinho** and **Roberto Firmino** to form an awesome attacking trio.

2016-17 HIGHLIGHTS

THE BEST BITS OF MANÉ'S FIRST SEASON WITH THE REDS.

14 AUGUST 2016

PREMIER LEAGUE

ARSENAL 3-4 LIVERPOOL

Not every player makes their debut in a **seven-goal thriller** *against Arsenal, but it happened to Sadio. His 63rd-minute goal turned out to be the winner!* **GO MANÉ!**

19 DECEMBER 2016

PREMIER LEAGUE

EVERTON 0-1 LIVERPOOL

Mané became a Liverpool hero with an injury-time winner in this, his first **Merseyside Derby.**

11 FEBRUARY 2017

PREMIER LEAGUE

LIVERPOOL 2-0 TOTTENHAM HOTSPUR

*Liverpool had not won in five games, but Mané single-handedly changed that with **TWO GOALS** in **two minutes** over an in-form Spurs.*

Mané was named as Liverpool's **Player of the Season!**

When **Mo Salah** joined the Reds at the start of the **2017–18** season, Liverpool had a **FAB FOUR** of forwards.

Mané, Salah and **Firmino** all scored in the opening game of the season. The trio had the making of something special.

Since playing together, Mané, Salah and Firmino have scored more than **270 goals** between them.

26 MAY 2018

CHAMPIONS LEAGUE FINAL

REAL MADRID 3-1 LIVERPOOL

After scoring against **Manchester City** and **Roma,** Sadio found himself in the Champions League **FINAL** against Real Madrid - a **HUGE** game!

Madrid took the lead early in the second half, only for our man Mané to equalise four minutes later!

BOOM!

Sadly, Madrid were the eventual winners, but Mané and his team-mates were determined to come back stronger.

Mané scored his first Liverpool **hat-trick** in **February 2018** against Porto in the **Champions League** round of 16.

Mané, Salah and Firmino each scored

10 GOALS

in the **2017–18 Champions League.**

AMAZING!

It was the **first time** three players from one club had each scored **10 Champions League Goals** in a single season.

CHAPTER 11

KINGS
OF
EUROPE

GOALS! GOALS! GOALS!

MANÉ HIT NEW GOALSCORING HEIGHTS IN THE PREMIER LEAGUE IN 2018-19.

12 AUGUST 2018

PREMIER LEAGUE

LIVERPOOL 4-0 WEST HAM

In the first game of the season Sadio scored a goal in each half. **Here. We. Go!**

27 FEBRUARY 2019

PREMIER LEAGUE

LIVERPOOL 5-0 WATFORD

Mané opened the scoring after **nine minutes** and followed it with the **cheekiest** backheel goal you've ever seen. **BOINK!**

10 MARCH 2019

PREMIER LEAGUE

LIVERPOOL 4-2 BURNLEY

Sadio's second goal was his **EIGHTH** in **SIX** home games and his **50th GOAL** for Liverpool.

Liverpool missed out on the *Premier League title* by just one point!

EUROPEAN DREAM

After seeing off both **Bayern Munich** (Mané scored twice) and **Barcelona** (a memorable 4-0 comeback) Liverpool reached the Champions League final once again.

1 JUNE 2019

CHAMPIONS LEAGUE FINAL

LIVERPOOL 2-0 TOTTENHAM HOTSPUR

Liverpool were ahead after just two minutes! A cross from Mané was handled in the box and the **penalty was scored** by Salah.

100

Divock Origi made it **2–0** and Liverpool had done it.

Mané **celebrated wildly** with his team-mates. The Ball Wizard from Bambali was now a

EUROPEAN CHAMPION!

GOLDEN GOALS

Liverpool did not win the Premier League that season, but Sadio was the League's joint top-scorer with **22 GOALS.**

He shared the **Golden Boot** with his team-mate **Mo Salah** and Arsenal striker **Pierre-Emerick Aubameyang**.

Aubameyang

CHAPTER 12

WE ARE THE CHAMPIONS

2019-20 HIGHLIGHTS

MANÉ'S BEST MOMENTS IN A VERY DIFFERENT SEASON.

14 AUGUST 2019

UEFA SUPER CUP

LIVERPOOL 2-2 CHELSEA (7-6 ON PENALTIES)

*Mané **scored** both Liverpool goals before the Reds finally overcame the Europa League winners. Sadio was **Man of the match.***

4 DECEMBER 2019

PREMIER LEAGUE

LIVERPOOL 5-2 EVERTON

*One goal and two assists from Mané in this Merseyside Derby helped Liverpool set a new club record: **unbeaten in 32 games.***

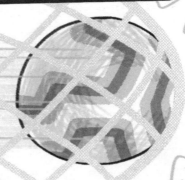

21 DECEMBER 2019

CLUB WORLD CUP

LIVERPOOL 1-0 FLAMENGO

*Mané assisted Firmino as Liverpool beat the Brazilians to be the **best club in the world!***

In **March 2020,** Liverpool were **25 POINTS** clear at the top of the league and on course to win their first league title for **30 YEARS.**

But then . . . all football stopped because of the **Coronavirus lockdown.**

WELL, ER . . . ALAS FOLKS WE'LL HAVE TO CANCEL THE FOOTBALL.

STAY HOME ▸ PROTECT THE NHS ▸ SAVE LIVES

ARCURI LECTERNS

The fans anxiously waited and hoped. Would Liverpool ever win the League again?

Finally, in June, the football came back - but the fans had to **stay at home.**

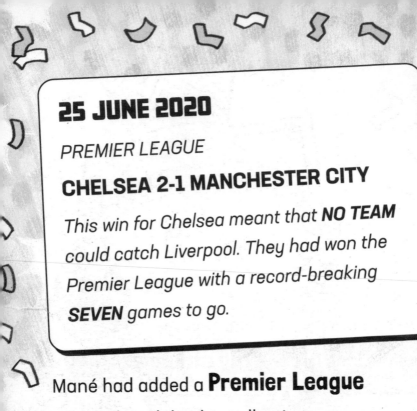

25 JUNE 2020

PREMIER LEAGUE

CHELSEA 2-1 MANCHESTER CITY

*This win for Chelsea meant that **NO TEAM** could catch Liverpool. They had won the Premier League with a record-breaking **SEVEN** games to go.*

Mané had added a **Premier League** winners' medal to his collection.

INCREDIBLE!

TOUGH TIMES

In the **2020–21** season, Sadio caught **Coronavirus** and missed some matches. His form dipped. Liverpool had some poor results.

Sadio said it was the **worst season** of his career!

But then . . . on the last day of the season against **Crystal Palace,** Sadio scored **both of Liverpool's goals** to secure **THIRD** place and all-important Champions League qualification.

HE WAS A KOP *HERO* ONCE MORE!

MANÉ LIVERPOOL STATS

SEASON	GAMES	GOALS	ASSISTS
2016-17	29	13	8
2017-18	44	20	9
2018-19	50	26	5
2019-20	47	22	12
2020-21	48	16	9

Wow, Sadio is a *great* player!

Yes! He scores *Mané goals!*

CHAPTER 13

WORLD ICON

STAR OF AFRICA

In **2019** Mané was voted **African Player of the Year.** His strike partner **Mo Salah** was second and Man City rival **Riyad Mahrez** came third.

The only other **Senegalese player** to win the award is Mané's hero **El Hadji Diouf.**

Sadio has scored **95 Premier League goals** – the most by a Senegalese player.

Mané is the only Senegalese player to score in a **Champions League final.**

BLAM!

FANTASTIC FORWARDS

Mané is one of the most valuable forwards in the world in **2021:**

SADIO MANÉ

CLUB: **LIVERPOOL**

COUNTRY: **SENEGAL**

EST VALUE: £90 MILLION

NEYMAR

CLUB: **PARIS SAINT-GERMAIN**

COUNTRY: **BRAZIL**

EST VALUE: **£99 MILLION**

ERLING HAALAND

CLUB: **BORUSSIA DORTMUND**

COUNTRY: **NORWAY**

EST VALUE: **£99 MILLION**

HARRY KANE

CLUB: **TOTTENHAM HOTSPUR**

COUNTRY: **ENGLAND**

EST VALUE: **£108 MILLION**

Sadio is one of the **biggest stars in world football,** but he has never forgotten his roots in Senegal. His family still live in Bambali and he visits home regularly.

He has paid for a **school** and a **hospital** to be built in the village . . .

HOPITAL DE BAMBALI

. . . and **donated money** to help the country during the coronavirus pandemic.

THANKS MANÉ!

MR NICE

Mané is known as one of the **nicest men in football.** Nobody has a bad word to say about him - and no wonder . . .

He gave his shirt to **ballboy** after winning the **UEFA Super Cup** . . .

THANKS!

MANÉ 10

Helped **unload water bottles** from the Senegal team bus . . .

And helped **clean the toilets** at his local **mosque.** (Liverpool had just beaten Leicester 2-1.)

WE LOVE YOU SADIO!

HONOURS AND RECORDS

HERE ARE A FEW OF THE MANY TROPHIES AND AWARDS MANÉ HAS COLLECTED:

AUSTRIAN BUNDESLIGA
2013-14

AUSTRIAN CUP
2013-14

PREMIER LEAGUE
2019-20

CHAMPIONS LEAGUE
2018-19

SUPER CUP
2019

CLUB WORLD CUP
2019

AFRICAN
FOOTBALLER
OF THE YEAR
2019

PLAYERS' PLAYER
OF THE YEAR
2016-17

PREMIER LEAGUE
GOLDEN BOOT
2018-19

PREMIER LEAGUE
PLAYER OF THE MONTH
AUGUST 2017
MARCH 2019
NOVEMBER 2019

QUIZ TIME!

How much do you know about **SADIO MANÉ**? Try this quiz to find out, then test your friends!

1. Which country is Mané from?

----

2. Which fruit did Sadio use to practise playing football?

----

3. Which Brazilian player was Sadio nicknamed in his village?

----

4. Which French club did Mané play for?

----

5. How much did Red Bull Salzburg pay for Mané in 2012?

----

6. Which team did Senegal beat 2-0 at the 2012 Olympics?

----

7. Mané scored three goals for Salzburg in a friendly against which German team?

----

8. When he was with Southampton, against which team did Sadio score the fastest Premier League hat-trick?

----

9. How many Liverpool goals did Mané score in 2018-19?

----

10. Which team did Liverpool beat to win the Champions League in 2019?

The answers are on the next page *but no peeking!*

ANSWERS

1. Senegal
2. Grapefruit
3. Ronaldinho
4. Metz
5. £3 million

6. Uruguay
7. Bayern Munich
8. Aston Villa
9. 26
10. Tottenham Hotspur

SADIO MANÉ:
WORDS YOU NEED TO KNOW

Premier League
The top football league in England.

Africa Cup of Nations
The main international football competition in Africa.

Austrian Bundesliga
The top football league in Austria.

Champions League
European club competition held every year. The winner is the best team in Europe.

Europa League
The second-tier European club competition.

ABOUT THE AUTHORS

Simon's first job was at the Science Museum, making paper aeroplanes and blowing bubbles big enough for your dad to stand in. Since then he's written all sorts of books about the stuff he likes, from dinosaurs and rockets, to llamas, loud music and of course, football. Simon has supported Ipswich Town since they won the FA Cup in 1978 (it's true - look it up) and once sat next to Rio Ferdinand on a train. He lives in Kent with his wife and daughter, a dog, cat and two tortoises.

Dan has drawn silly pictures since he could hold a crayon. Then he grew up and started making books about stuff like trucks, space, people's jobs, *Doctor Who* and *Star Wars*. Dan remembers Ipswich Town winning the FA Cup but he didn't watch it because he was too busy making a Viking ship out of brown paper. As a result, he knows more about Vikings than football. Dan lives in Suffolk with his wife, son, daughter and a dog that takes him for very long walks.